INVESTIGATING SCIENCE CHALLENGES

Investigating SOUND

Richard Spilsbury

CRABTREE
PUBLISHING COMPANY
WWW.CRABTREEBOOKS.COM

CRABTREE
PUBLISHING COMPANY
WWW.CRABTREEBOOKS.COM

Author: Richard Spilsbury

Editors: Sarah Eason, Jennifer Sanderson, Petrice Custance, Reagan Miller

Proofreaders: Kris Hirschmann, Janine Deschenes

Indexer: Wendy Scavuzzo

Editorial director: Kathy Middleton

Design: Emma DeBanks

Cover design and additional artwork: Emma DeBanks

Photo research: Rachel Blount

Production coordinator and prepress technician: Tammy McGarr

Print coordinator: Katherine Berti

Consultant: David Hawksett

Produced for Crabtree Publishing Company by Calcium Creative

Photo Credits:

t=Top, tr=Top Right, tl=Top Left

Inside: Shutterstock: Antoniodiaz: pp. 24-25; ASuruwataRi: pp. 14-15; Willyam Bradberry: pp. 8-9; Carlos Castilla: pp. 1, 26-27; Designua: p. 9t; Aleksandar Grozdanovski: p. 14c; Kurhan: p. 19; LuckyImages: pp. 22-23; Boris Medvedev: p. 14bl; Dudarev Mikhail: p. 7t; Monkey Business Images: p. 25b; Nahlik: p. 22b; Paulaphoto: p. 15r; Pretty Vectors: p. 18; Rawpixel.com: pp. 4-5; Vadim Sadovski: pp. 6-7; Keith Usher: p. 13b; Vvvita: p. 13t; Debby Wong: p. 5t.

Cover: Tudor Photography.

Library and Archives Canada Cataloguing in Publication

Spilsbury, Richard, 1963-, author.
Investigating sound / Richard Spilsbury.

(Investigating science challenges)
Includes index.
Issued in print and electronic formats.
ISBN 978-0-7787-4209-8 (hardcover).--
ISBN 978-0-7787-4380-4 (softcover).--
ISBN 978-1-4271-2013-7 (HTML)

1. Sound--Juvenile literature. 2. Sound-waves--Juvenile literature.
3. Sound--Experiments--Juvenile literature. I. Title.

QC225.5.S695 2018   j534   C2017-907744-9
                                             C2017-907745-7

Library of Congress Cataloging-in-Publication Data

Names: Spilsbury, Richard, 1963- author.
Title: Investigating sound / Richard Spilsbury.
Description: New York, New York : Crabtree Publishing, [2018] | Series: Investigating science challenges | Includes index.
Identifiers: LCCN 2017059671 (print) | LCCN 2017060342 (ebook) | ISBN 9781427120137 (Electronic HTML) | ISBN 9780778742098 (reinforced library binding) | ISBN 9780778743804 (pbk.)
Subjects: LCSH: Sound--Juvenile literature. | Sound-waves--Juvenile literature. | Sound--Experiments--Juvenile literature.
Classification: LCC QC225.5 (ebook) | LCC QC225.5 .S66954 2018 (print) | DDC 534--dc23
LC record available at https://lccn.loc.gov/2017059671

Crabtree Publishing Company

www.crabtreebooks.com   1-800-387-7650

Printed in the U.S.A./022018/CG20171220

Published in Canada
Crabtree Publishing
616 Welland Ave.
St. Catharines, Ontario
L2M 5V6

Published in the United States
Crabtree Publishing
PMB 59051
350 Fifth Avenue, 59th Floor
New York, New York 10118

Published in the United Kingdom
Crabtree Publishing
Maritime House
Basin Road North, Hove
BN41 1WR

Published in Australia
Crabtree Publishing
3 Charles Street
Coburg North
VIC, 3058

CONTENTS

A World of Sound.................................4

Sounds on the Move..........................6

How Sound Travels.............................8

Let's Investigate: Bag of Sound.........10

Looking at Sound Waves....................12

Changing Pitch..................................14

Let's Investigate: Pitch Perfect..........16

Hearing Sounds................................18

Let's Investigate: Loud Mouth............20

Reflecting and Absorbing..................22

Using Sound Energy..........................24

Investigate More...............................26

Science Challenge Tips......................28

Glossary..30

Learning More.................................31

Index and About the Author..............32

A WORLD OF SOUND

We live in a world of sound. From the beeping of the alarm clock that wakes us up in the morning to the click of the light switch that we turn off at bedtime, sounds provide the backdrop to our whole lives. Sounds help us **communicate**, learn, understand the world around us, and stay safe. Sounds are important because they can tell us what is happening around us even when we cannot see what is making the sound.

Sounds are all around us wherever we go. We hear sounds up close or in the distance.

Sound Energy

Sound is a form of **energy**. Energy is the power or ability to make things move, work, or happen. There are many forms of energy. For example, the Sun gives out light and heat energy, which helps us see and stay warm. Sound is a form of energy that you can hear with your ears.

Good Vibrations

Sound energy is made when objects **vibrate**. To vibrate means to move quickly back and forth with very short, repeated movements. An object vibrates when a **force** acts on it. A force is a push or a pull. When you pluck a guitar string, it vibrates and the vibrating string makes the air around it vibrate, too. The vibrating air carries the sounds to our ears so we can hear the guitar playing.

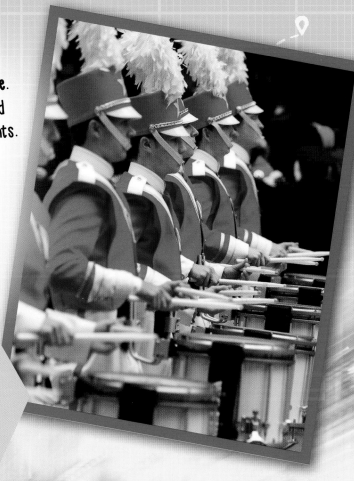

When the drums vibrate after being struck with sticks, they produce the sound energy we hear.

INVESTIGATE

Scientists **observe** the world around them and ask questions. They then plan and carry out **investigations** to find answers. In this book, you will carry out investigations to answer questions about sound. On pages 28 and 29 you can find investigation tips, check your work, and read suggestions for other investigations you can try.

SOUNDS ON THE MOVE

Things that vibrate and make noises are called **sources** of sound. A dog barking, a bell ringing, and leaves rustling are all sources of sound. When you speak, touch your throat and you will be able to feel the vibrations of your **vocal cords**. These are also a source of sound.

Sound Waves

Energy is useful because it can be carried from one place to another. Sound energy travels in **waves**. Waves are regular patterns of motion. You cannot see sound waves, but they are all around you. They travel out from a source in all directions. Even though you might not be able to see the source of a sound, such as a dog barking, you can hear it when its sound waves reach you!

In space, it is completely silent. This is because there is no air between the planets, stars, and other space objects. Without air, there is nothing to pass on vibrations, so sound waves cannot travel in space.

Sound waves travel outward from the source of the sound in all directions, similar to the way ripples spread out in repeating circles when you drop a rock into a pond.

Sound Matters

We usually hear noises when sound waves travel to our ears through the air, which is a type of **gas**. Sound waves can also travel through **liquids** such as water, and **solids** such as metal and wood. Solids, liquids, and gases are different types of **matter**. Matter is any substance or material that takes up space, even if we cannot see it, as in the case of air. A **medium** is any matter that passes on energy. You can hear sounds through different mediums. For example, you hear sounds when a friend calls to you through the air from across a field, knocks on your solid wooden front door from outside, or talks to you when you are swimming underwater.

7

HOW SOUND TRAVELS

Sound waves move through matter by vibrating the **atoms** and **molecules** in a solid, liquid, or gas. Atoms are the tiny **particles** that make up all living and nonliving things. Molecules are tiny groups of atoms bonded together, which combine in different ways. Molecules can be seen only with a powerful microscope but they are in you, your clothes, your computer, and your lunch. When a molecule vibrates, its movement makes the molecules nearby vibrate as well, helping the sound waves move through matter.

Whales make sounds to communicate with one another. Their sounds travel over huge distances through ocean waters.

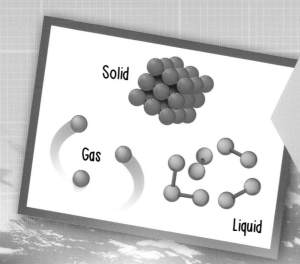

Solid

Gas

Liquid

This image shows the positioning of molecules in the three different states of matter—solid, liquid, and gas.

Moving Molecules

Sound waves move differently through different types of material because of the way their molecules are spaced out. Solid objects, such as metal, have many molecules packed closely together. Molecules in liquids are spread out a little more, and in gases the molecules are spread out even farther from one another. Sound travels fast through a metal such as steel, because its molecules can pass sound energy to nearby molecules quickly. In a gas such as air, the molecules are more spread out, so it takes more time for sound waves to move between them.

INVESTIGATE

You can see how quickly different objects can pass on movements by setting up three long rows of dominoes. You could make one row close together, the other a little farther apart, and the last one even farther apart, but just close enough that they can knock down the next domino in line when they fall. Which row of dominoes do you think will fall the most quickly? Which will be slowest? Explain your thinking.

BAG OF SOUND

The different ways molecules are arranged in solids, liquids, and gases affects the speed at which sounds can move through them. For example, do you notice how the speed at which sounds move changes when you make a noise in water or in air? Let's investigate how sound travels through different mediums.

Step 1: Seal the zipper of the ziplock bag, leaving just a small gap in the middle. Blow into the bag through the gap and quickly seal it to create a puffed bag of air.

Step 2: Hold the bag over your ear so it covers the opening of the ear. Ask your friend to tap the bag with the blunt end of a pencil. Listen to the sound and describe its volume, or how loud or soft it is.

Step 3: Next, fill the bag with water and zip it shut tightly. Repeat step 2, and be careful not to burst the bag. How does it sound now?

Step 4: Now repeat step 3 but substitute the bag for the solid wooden block. Would you expect the sound of the pencil tap to be louder or softer than it is through the water-filled bag? Remember what you have learned in this book about sound waves and the mediums they move through.

THINK!

Challenge Questions

- Was your prediction correct?
- Was there a difference in the loudness of the sound you heard through air, water, and wood? If so, what do you think caused this variation?
- Which medium produced the loudest sound and which one made the softest sound?
- Why is it important for your friend to tap the bag with the pencil using the same amount of force each time?

LOOKING AT SOUND WAVES

From a loud bang to a soft whisper, or the low rumble of a foghorn to the high shriek of a whistle, our ears can hear a huge variety of sound. Sounds differ because of the kind of sound waves made by a vibrating source. Images of sound waves show them moving up and down, similar to an ocean wave. The height of the sound wave is the distance between the center of the wave and its highest or lowest points. This is called the wave's **amplitude**. The distance between any two high points of a wave, called **crests,** or any two low points of a wave, called **troughs,** is called its **wavelength.**

Loud and Soft

If you hit a drum hard, the vibrations of the drum skin are bigger. The amplitude of the sound wave is large. We say it has a higher **volume.** When the sound wave amplitude is large, there is a loud sound. If you hit the drum more gently, it makes smaller vibrations. With smaller amplitude, the sounds are quieter and have a lower volume.

High and Low

The pitch of a sound, or whether it is high or low, depends on how quickly an object vibrates. When a string on a guitar vibrates very quickly, it plays a high-pitched sound. When it vibrates very slowly, it plays a low-pitched sound. The number of times an object vibrates every second is called the **frequency** of the sound. A high-pitched sound vibrates many times each second, so it has a high frequency. Low-pitched sounds have a low frequency. Smoke alarms vibrate about 3,000 times a second to make a very high-pitched, piercing sound so everyone hears the noise. This warning tells us to get away from the source of the smoke, such as a fire.

A kitten makes a soft but high, squeaky sound. Many vibrations per second (a high frequency) make a high sound. Short vibrations (less amplitude) make a soft sound.

amplitude

time

Sound waves are invisible, but we can show them as wiggly lines so that we can see how different kinds of vibrations make different sounds.

A lion makes a loud, rumbling, deep roar.

amplitude

time

Few vibrations per second (a low frequency) make a low sound. Tall vibrations (more amplitude) make a loud sound.

13

CHANGING PITCH

Any piece of music, from an orchestral symphony to a best-selling hit, is a pattern of sounds of different pitch. Different instruments make sounds of different pitch. For example, a kettle drum has a lower pitch than a snare drum when a player hits it. Generally, the smaller a vibrating object is, the easier it is to vibrate with greater frequency, resulting in a higher pitch.

snare drum

kettle drum

The long bars on a xylophone vibrate more slowly than the short bars, so the long bars make a lower-pitched sound.

The Thing About Strings

String size also matters for pitch. Long strings vibrate more slowly, have a lower frequency, and make lower-pitched sounds than short strings. That is why the strings on a large double bass play much lower pitches than a violin. Many stringed instruments have several strings of the same length, but with different thicknesses. Their thickest strings vibrate slowest, with the lowest frequency and pitch, whereas the thinnest strings make the highest-pitched sounds. A thin string will have a frequency and pitch twice as high as one with twice its diameter, or twice as thick.

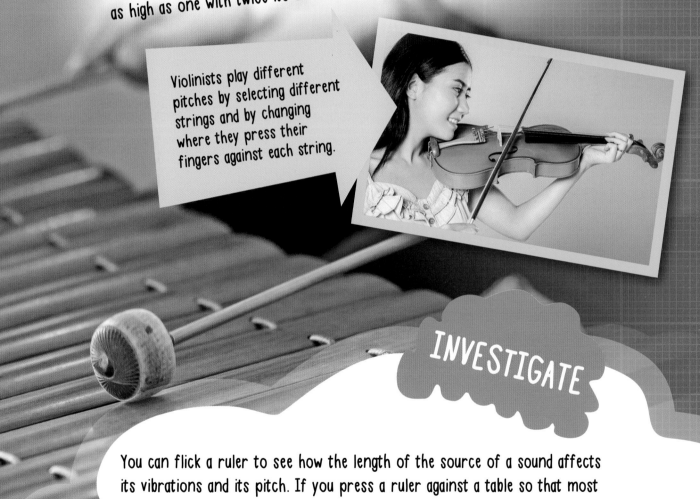

Violinists play different pitches by selecting different strings and by changing where they press their fingers against each string.

INVESTIGATE

You can flick a ruler to see how the length of the source of a sound affects its vibrations and its pitch. If you press a ruler against a table so that most of it hangs off into the air, and then push down on the free end quickly, it should vibrate and make a sound. Do you think the sound will be different if you shorten the part of the ruler that is hanging off the table and vibrating? Which sound will be higher and which will be lower? Why?

PITCH PERFECT

People can produce sounds of different pitch from a guitar by using different strings. Have you noticed how guitarists also move their fingers along the strings from top to bottom as they play music? Why are they doing this? Let's investigate pitch by making lower- and higher-pitched sounds.

You Will Need:

- 4 large rubber bands of the same length, but each with a different width
- A 12-inch- (30-cm-) long shallow oven tray
- A 12-inch (30-cm) ruler
- Modeling clay

Step 1: Stretch the rubber bands around the tray, in order from narrowest to widest. Leave gaps of around 1 inch (2.5 cm) between each rubber band.

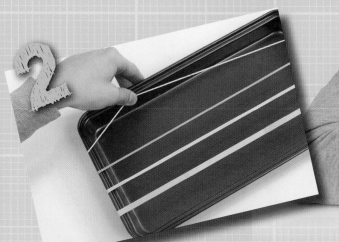

Step 2: Pull and let go of each string in turn. Try to use the same force each time. Can you hear a different pitch each time?

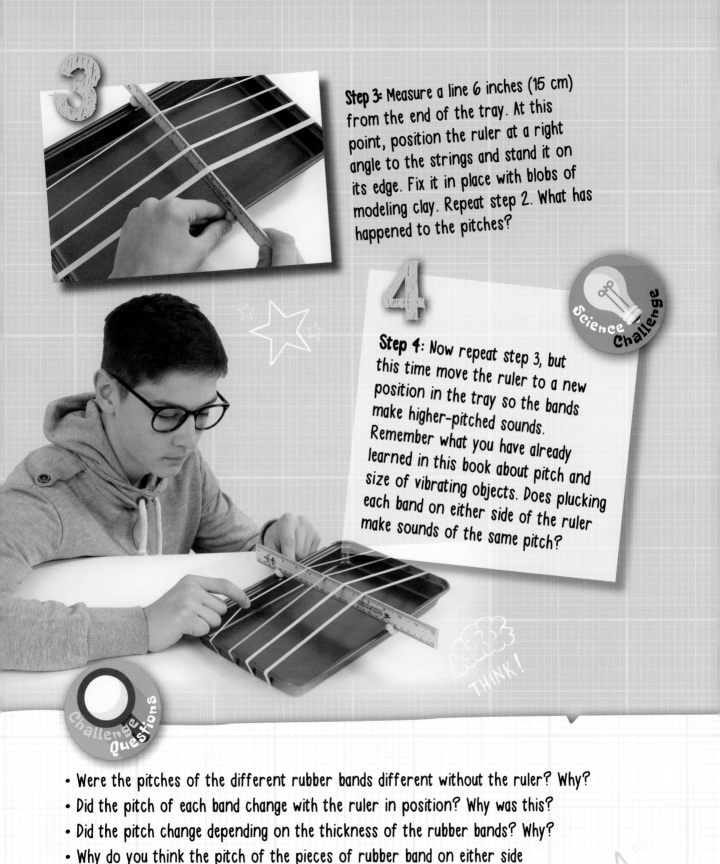

Step 3: Measure a line 6 inches (15 cm) from the end of the tray. At this point, position the ruler at a right angle to the strings and stand it on its edge. Fix it in place with blobs of modeling clay. Repeat step 2. What has happened to the pitches?

Step 4: Now repeat step 3, but this time move the ruler to a new position in the tray so the bands make higher-pitched sounds. Remember what you have already learned in this book about pitch and size of vibrating objects. Does plucking each band on either side of the ruler make sounds of the same pitch?

Science Challenge

THINK!

Challenge Questions

- Were the pitches of the different rubber bands different without the ruler? Why?
- Did the pitch of each band change with the ruler in position? Why was this?
- Did the pitch change depending on the thickness of the rubber bands? Why?
- Why do you think the pitch of the pieces of rubber band on either side of the ruler were different?

HEARING SOUNDS

We hear sounds when sound waves reach our ears. The outer parts of the ears, on the sides of your head, are shaped to collect sound waves. They funnel the waves inside the ear so we can hear the sounds.

How Ears Work

Sound waves enter our ears by entering the hole and traveling along a short tunnel called the **ear canal**. When they hit a thin piece of stretched skin called the **eardrum** at the end of the canal, they make it vibrate. The eardrum transfers the vibrations to three tiny bones called **ossicles**. The vibrations move through the ossicles to a small, snail-shaped tube called the **cochlea**, which is filled with liquid and lined with thousands of tiny hairs. The hairs vibrate when waves move through the liquid. The vibrations trigger electrical signals that travel to the brain. The brain interprets these signals and tells us what the sounds are.

Sound waves in air convert to vibrations in the eardrum, ossicles, and cochlea. Information about the frequency and amplitude of sounds then gets passed on to the brain

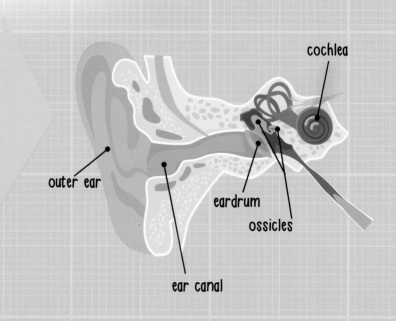

cochlea

outer ear

eardrum

ossicles

ear canal

18

Sounds become quieter the farther they travel because they run out of energy. Loud noises travel farther because they have more energy to start with.

Listen Up!

Our ears can hear loud sounds from far away because these sounds have a lot of energy. We use more energy to shout than we do to whisper. This means the sound waves have more energy to make molecules ahead of them vibrate, so the sound can travel farther. Yet even loud sounds stop eventually. As sound waves move farther from their source, they gradually run out of energy. The vibrations become smaller and smaller. The sound gets quieter until it stops.

INVESTIGATE

Outer ears capture some sound waves, but larger funnel shapes capture more energy. That is why we cup our hands around our ears. The extra funnel shape of our hands redirect more of the spreading sound waves in toward our ear so we can hear sounds from farther away. What happens when we cup our hands around our mouths to make sounds louder? Do you think it makes a difference if our hands make a smaller or larger funnel shape?

Let's Investigate

LOUD MOUTH

You Will Need:

- A pencil
- 2 large sheets of stiff paper
- A small plate
- A pair of scissors
- Tape
- A large plate
- A friend
- A playing field or large open area

When sound waves spread out as they travel through a medium such as air, they lose their energy. Making a funnel shape helps direct the sound waves in one direction so people in that direction can hear it better. Megaphones are cone-shaped devices that allow people to project their voices over long distances without having to yell. How does the size of a megaphone affect how it works? Let's investigate sound and distance by making megaphones.

Step 1: Draw around the small plate onto the paper. Cut out the circle of paper. Fold it in half. Then cut along the fold line to make a semicircle of paper.

Step 2: Make a megaphone by pulling and rolling the corners of the semicircle together to make a cone shape. Tape along the seam. There should be a small hole at the narrow end of the cone. If not, cut off the tip. Repeat steps 1 and 2 with the large plate to make a bigger megaphone.

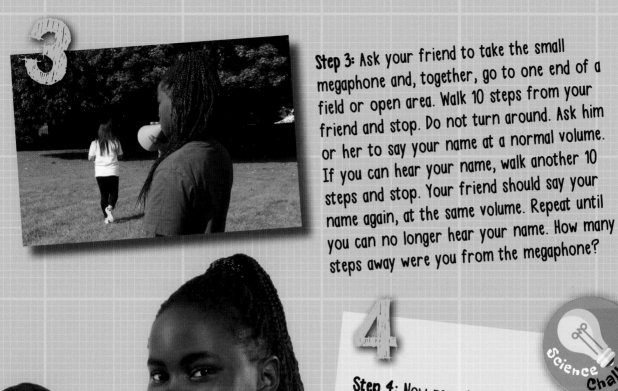

Step 3: Ask your friend to take the small megaphone and, together, go to one end of a field or open area. Walk 10 steps from your friend and stop. Do not turn around. Ask him or her to say your name at a normal volume. If you can hear your name, walk another 10 steps and stop. Your friend should say your name again, at the same volume. Repeat until you can no longer hear your name. How many steps away were you from the megaphone?

Step 4: Now repeat step 3, but this time decide on what to use to help you hear your friend from farther away. Your friend could use the larger megaphone or no megaphone. Remember what you have learned about how sounds lose energy and amplitude with distance from the source. Then try the other alternative to see what happens.

Science Challenge

Challenge Questions

- When using the large megaphone, then no megaphone at all, was there a difference in the number of steps you took before you could not hear your name?
- Did the large megaphone work better than the small megaphone at amplifying your friend's voice? If so, why?
- Why is it important for your friend to speak at the same volume for each test?

REFLECTING AND ABSORBING

Have you ever noticed that the space in which a sound is made can affect the sound? Sound waves can travel through different forms of matter, but they can also be **reflected** off them. When sound waves hit a hard, flat surface, they reflect and bounce back in the direction of the source of the sound, similar to a ball bouncing off a wall. In large, empty spaces with hard surfaces all around, such as a cave or canyon, the sound waves reflect back so well that they cause **echoes**.

Absorbing Sound

Some objects and surfaces **absorb**, or soak up, sound waves instead of reflecting them. Soft, bumpy surfaces are the opposite of hard, smooth surfaces; because they absorb rather than reflect the energy in sound waves. That is why your voice may echo when you shout out in an empty room, but it will not echo if that same room is filled with curtains, carpets, and sofas.

Reflective panels on the ceilings and sides of a modern concert hall can spread musical sounds throughout the hall evenly.

Using sound-absorbing materials in a recording studio prevents outside noise from being picked up by a singer's **microphones**, and ending up on the album!

Acoustics

The way sound travels in a room is called its **acoustics**. Musicians may alter the acoustics of a room to control the way sound is reflected or absorbed. Concert halls are large buildings. They often have hard and smooth panels over the walls and ceilings that help reflect sound waves toward the audience so they can hear the music more clearly and loudly. In a recording studio, walls may be covered with materials that absorb sound. This stops sounds getting in from outside that could wreck a band's carefully rehearsed recording.

USING SOUND ENERGY

A megaphone amplifies sounds a little, but to get a really loud sound, people use electric machines. Microphones capture energy in sound waves and convert the waves into patterns of electrical energy that copy the amplitude and frequency of the sound. **Amplifiers** keep the same frequency, so pitch does not change, but they increase the amplitude. Then **loudspeakers** change electrical signals into louder sounds. When the electrical energy is changed into sound energy, no energy is lost. It is simply transferred or moved from one form to another.

Going Farther

Sound waves lose energy over long distances, but you can always use a cell phone to talk to a friend in another place. When you talk into a cell phone, the phone instantly converts the sound waves into **radio waves**. Radio waves are a type of energy that can travel a very long way through the air. The phone sends the radio waves to a cell tower near you. The cell tower relays them to a base station that sends them to another cell tower and then to your friend's phone, which converts the radio waves back into sound waves.

Mini loudspeakers in earbud headphones enlarge the tiny amplitudes of recorded music on MP3 players or cell phones into full, rich sounds.

24

Seeing with Sound

Ultrasound is very high-frequency sound waves with a pitch far beyond what humans can hear. Ultrasound waves can travel fast through liquids and be used to see what is inside liquids. Ultrasound waves bounce back in echoes when they hit a solid object in a liquid. Machines produce an image based on how much energy is reflected back. Ultrasound is used on boats to spot schools of fish or shipwrecks on the sea floor. It is also used by doctors to see how babies are developing inside their mothers' wombs.

Ultrasound waves move from a machine through a mother's stomach wall, and echo back from the child inside.

INVESTIGATE MORE

Complete silence is a very rare experience. Even when sitting in a quiet classroom, there are always noises, from the whir of machines such as fans inside computers to muffled voices in the hallway and passing traffic outside. On a busy train, many people try to block out the sounds around them by turning up the volume on their headphones. This can be a big mistake.

Sound Danger

People measure the loudness or amplitude of sound waves in units called decibels. Many young people can hear sounds as quiet as 1 decibel and as loud as 140 decibels. The background noise in most homes measures around 40 decibels, and normal talking is 60 decibels. However, sounds louder than 90 decibels, such as your favorite song being played loudly, can cause ear damage. Constant large amplitudes put stress on the sensitive parts inside ears. People can reduce sound danger by keeping their distance from loud sound sources, turning down the volume, or by wearing ear protection. Do some research on your own to learn how musicians stop their own ears from becoming damaged from loud instruments, while still being able to hear the music they are playing.

Using headphones at the maximum volume can measure 105 decibels. Working in the music industry, where this volume is common, can damage a person's hearing.

Preventing Noise Pollution

Permanent moderate to loud background noise, such as the hum of constant traffic on highways or the distant roar of airplanes coming and going from airports, is often called noise pollution. Noise pollution can prevent people from sleeping, make it difficult to concentrate at work or school, and increase stress levels. One way to reduce noise pollution is to add sound-absorbing materials to windows. Can you think of other ways people prevent noise pollution?

INVESTIGATE

People talk and sing by vibrating their vocal cords. Other animals make sounds in many different ways. Investigate how the following animals make sounds to communicate with others: grasshoppers, frogs, rattlesnakes, songbirds, and blue whales. Dolphins, bats, and moths hunt using ultrasound. How do they do this?

Science Challenge TIPS

Pages 10–11: Bag of Sound

You should have heard differences in the loudness of sound depending on the material. You could probably hear the loudest sound of the tapping pencil through the wood. The closely packed molecules in this solid medium transfer sound energy much more easily and rapidly than the liquid medium. Sound waves pass slowest through air, the gas medium, so this made the softest sound.

To make the investigation fair, it is important to try to tap with the same force so that the same amount of sound energy passes through each medium.

Pages 16–17: Pitch Perfect

Without the ruler, the wider, heavier rubber bands should make lower-pitched sounds than the narrower, lighter bands. That is because narrower materials generally vibrate with a higher frequency than thicker ones. You should find that when the ruler is moved to the 6 inch (15 cm) position, the pitch of each band changes. The length of band that can vibrate is halved from 12 inches (30 cm) to 6 inches (15 cm) in length, so the frequency of vibration doubles. This means that the pitch is twice as high. We can make the pitch even higher by shifting the ruler closer toward one end of the tray than the other. However, it depends on which side of the ruler the bands are plucked. The shorter piece of band makes a higher pitch than the longer piece.

Investigate stringed instruments such as the harp, violin, and double bass. How does the length of their strings affect their pitch?

Page 20-21: Loud Mouth

You will probably hear your name from the greatest distance when your friend uses the larger megaphone and the shortest distance when no megaphone is used. Normally, sound waves spread in all directions from their source. A megaphone traps and stacks up the sound waves. This gives them greater amplitude and stops the spread of sound energy. The sound is louder and more of the waves are going in the same direction, so the sound travels farther.

With a large megaphone, there is a greater amount of air for vibrations from the vocal cords to stack up than in the smaller megaphone, so it produces a louder sound.

Your friend should speak at the same volume for each test to make the investigation fair.

Investigate further by cupping your hands around your ears and redoing the test. Does this help you to hear the sounds? Can you explain why this is?

GLOSSARY

Some bold-faced words are defined
where they appear in the text.

absorb Soak up

acoustics The way that sounds travel

amplifiers Devices used to increase the amplitude or loudness of a sound

amplitude The height of a wave, measured from its center or resting position

atoms The tiny particles that make up everything. Atoms are so small that we cannot see them.

cochlea A tube in the inner ear lined with hairs that vibrate and send signals to the brain

communicate To share information

crests The peaks or top points of waves

ear canal The tube that carries sound from outside into the ear

eardrum The part of the ear that vibrates and moves tiny bones inside the ear, called ossicles

echoes Sounds caused by sound waves reflecting off hard surfaces

energy Ability or power to do work

force The effect that causes things to move in a particular way, usually a push or a pull

frequency Number of regular movements in a given amount of time

gas A substance that is often invisible. It does not keep its shape or always take up the same amount of space.

investigations Procedures carried out to observe, study, or test something to learn more about it

liquids Substances that can be poured and take the shape of the container they are in. Liquids always take up the same amount of space

loudspeakers Devices that change electrical signals into sound waves

matter Any physical thing that takes up space, such as air and wood

medium Any matter that carries waves of energy

microphones Devices that change sound waves into electrical signals

observe To use your senses to gather information

ossicles The three tiny bones in the middle ear that vibrate and move sound to the cochlea

particles Extremely tiny pieces of material

radio waves A type of energy that can carry sounds long distances

reflected Bounced or thrown back

solids Substances that keep their shape and always take up the same amount of space

sources Places, people, or things from which something originates or can be obtained

troughs The lowest points of waves

vibrate Repeatedly move up and down very quickly

vocal cords The parts of the throat that help people make sounds with their voice

volume Loudness of a sound

wavelength The distance between two crests or two troughs of a wave

waves Disturbances carrying energy through water, air, or other mediums

LEARNING MORE

Find out more about sound and its uses.

Books

Canavan, Thomas. *Super Experiments with Light and Sound* (Mind-Blowing Science Experiments). Gareth Stevens, 2017.

Johnson, Robin. *The Science of Sound Waves* (Catch a Wave). Crabtree Publishing Company, 2017.

Loria, Laura. *What Is Sound Energy?* (Let's Find Out! Forms of Energy). Britannica Educational Publishing in Association with Rosen Education, 2017.

Riley, Peter. *Sound* (Moving Up With Science). PowerKids Press, 2017.

Websites

There is an easy-to-understand introduction to the science of sound at:
www.explainthatstuff.com/sound.html

Learn about the instruments of the orchestra and how they make different sounds at:
http://artsalive.ca/en/mus/instrumentlab

Try this fun activity to make sound waves at:
www.scientificamerican.com/article/making-sound-waves

Find out more about science at:
http://idahoptv.org/sciencetrek/topics/sound/facts.cfm

INDEX

A
absorption 22–23
acoustics 23
air 5, 6–7, 9, 10–11, 15, 18, 20, 24, 28–29
amplifiers 24
amplitude 12–13, 18, 21, 24, 26, 29
atoms 8

B
brain 18

C
cell phones 24
changing energy 24
cochlea 18
concert halls 22–23
crests 12

D
double bass 15, 29
drum 5, 12, 14

E
ear canal 18
eardrum 18
ears 4–5, 7, 10, 12, 18–19, 26, 29
echoes 22, 25
electrical energy 24
energy defined 4
experiments 10–11, 16–17, 20–21, 28–29

F
force 5, 11, 16, 28
frequency 12–13, 14–15, 18, 24–25, 28

G
gas 7, 8–9, 10, 28
guitar 5, 12, 16

H
headphones 24, 26–27
hearing sounds 4–5, 6–7, 11, 12, 16, 18–19, 20–21, 23, 25, 26–27, 28–29
heat energy 4

I
investigations 5, 9, 10–11, 15, 16–17, 19, 20–21, 26–27, 28–29

L
light energy 4
liquids 7, 8–9, 10, 18, 25, 28
loudness 11, 26, 28
loud sounds 11, 12–13, 19, 23, 24, 26–27, 28–29
loudspeakers 24

M
matter 7, 8–9, 22
measuring sound 26–27
medium 7, 10–11, 20, 28
megaphones 20–21, 24, 29
metal 7, 9
microphones 23, 24
molecules 8–9, 10, 19, 28
moving sound 6–7, 8–9, 10–11, 18–19, 20, 22–23, 25, 29
music 14, 16, 22–23, 24, 26–27

N
noise pollution 27

O
ossicles 18

P
particles 8, 9
pitch 12, 14–15, 16–17, 24–25, 28–29

Q
quiet/soft sounds 11, 12–13, 19, 26, 28

R
radio waves 24
recording studio 23
reflection 22–23, 25

S
solids 7, 8–9, 10, 25, 28
sound waves 6–7, 8–9, 11, 12–13, 18–19, 20, 22–23, 24–25, 26, 28–29

sources of sound 6, 7, 12, 15, 19, 21, 22, 26, 29
states of matter 9
strings 5, 12, 15, 16–17, 29

T
troughs 12

U
ultrasound 25, 27

V
vibrations 5, 6, 8, 12–13, 14–15, 17, 18–19, 27, 28–29
vocal cords 6, 27, 29
volume 12, 21, 26–27, 29

W
wavelength 12

About the AUTHOR

Richard Spilsbury has a science degree, and has had a lifelong fascination with science. He has written and co-written many books for young people on a wide variety of topics, from ants to avalanches.